Budgie Care Manual:
A Book on How to Care
for Budgies for the Beginners

Step-by-Step Instructions for Selecting, Grooming, and Maintaining a Happy, Healthy Budgie – Complete with Practical Tips, Essential Resources, and Proven Methods for Parakeet Owners

By Budgie Press

Budgie Care Manual: A Book on How to Care for Budgies for the Beginners
© 2024 Budgie Press

Disclaimer

The information provided in this (book/eBook) is designed to offer helpful information on the subjects discussed. It is not intended as a substitute for professional advice. The views and opinions expressed in this book are solely those of the author and do not necessarily reflect the official policy or position of any organization or entity.

Readers are advised to consult with a qualified professional for any advice pertaining to specific situations or conditions discussed herein. The author disclaims any liability arising directly or indirectly from the use of this book.

Dedicated to

To all the budgies who brighten our days with their chirps, their cheeky antics, and their boundless curiosity. And to the pet parents who love them like family – you make the world a warmer, brighter place, one tiny feather at a time.

Preface

You're thinking about getting a budgie, huh? Or maybe you already have one – and you're here because you want to be the best budgie parent possible. Either way, you've come to the right place. I'm here to share all the secrets, tips, and advice I've picked up along the way, so that you can enjoy every feathered moment of life with your little companion.

Let's be real for a second: owning a budgie isn't just about feeding them seeds and cleaning out their cage (although, that's important too!). It's about building a connection with a tiny creature that's more than just a bird. They've got personalities that can rival the quirkiest of humans. Some days, your budgie will be the life of the party, chirping away like it's auditioning for a role on Broadway. Other days, they'll be cuddled up in a corner, giving you the side-eye like you've done something terribly wrong (spoiler: you haven't).

That's what I love most about budgies. They're *alive* in a way that you might not expect from a little bird. They'll keep you on your toes, make you laugh, and sometimes leave you wondering, "Did that just happen?" But don't worry – I'm here to guide you through the highs and lows of budgie ownership, with plenty of heart and humor along the way.

This book is more than just a manual; it's your personal companion in this beautiful journey of budgie love. You'll find practical tips, how-tos, and checklists to help you take care of your budgie, as well as some deep dives into their behavior and needs. But it's also filled with stories, personal insights, and a whole lot of heart – because, let's face it, being a pet owner is as much about feeling connected to your little friend as it is about knowing what kind of food to buy.

Does that make sense? I hope so. But just in case it doesn't, don't worry – I've got your back. Whether you're here for the basics or you're looking to become the bird whisperer you were always meant to be, this book will walk you through every step with warmth, wit, and a little bit of sass.

Now, grab a cup of tea (or whatever beverage suits your fancy) and get comfy. Your budgie journey starts here. And trust me, it's going to be a ride you won't want to miss.

Table of Contents

Welcome to Budgie Care

So, you've decided to bring a budgie into your life. First off, congratulations! These tiny, colorful birds can quickly become more than just pets – they can become companions, little characters that light up your day with their quirky antics and sweet chirps. But I get it – taking on the care of a budgie can feel like stepping into unknown territory, especially if you're new to bird ownership. That's where this guide comes in. Think of it as your friendly road map through the wonderful (and sometimes hilariously unpredictable) world of budgies. We're going to cover everything you need to know, from setting up their home to understanding their moods and behaviors, and even a few tips on how to get them to talk to you (yes, it's possible!).

Why Choose a Budgie as a Pet?

Now, you might be wondering: why budgies? Well, for starters, they're small, low-maintenance, and full of personality. A budgie doesn't need a mansion-sized cage or an elaborate daily routine to thrive – in fact, they're quite content with a simple setup and the occasional bit of attention. But don't be fooled by their size; these little guys are like the extroverts of the bird world. They're curious, playful, and incredibly social, which makes them fantastic companions. They'll keep you company when you're working, sing you a tune when you're feeling low, and provide endless entertainment with their energetic flights around the house.

And let's not forget, budgies are one of the few pets that don't require you to break the bank for supplies. If you've ever looked at the cost of owning a dog or a cat, you know what I mean. But with budgies? You're talking about a bird who's perfectly happy with a few toys, a perch, and a regular supply of seeds. They're pocket-friendly and can still bring joy into your life in a big way.

Understanding Your Budgie's Behavior

But here's the thing – to truly get the most out of your relationship with your budgie, you need to understand them. And trust me, budgies are *smart*. They're not just sitting in that cage twiddling their feathers; they're constantly observing, thinking, and reacting to their environment. The trick is learning their language.

When your budgie is chirping away at 6 AM (yes, before the sun even comes up – they're early risers), don't assume they're just making noise for the sake of it. That's them calling out to you, telling you they're awake and ready to start their day. Or when they bob their heads up and down like they're grooving to their favorite song? That's a sign of happiness, a little birdie dance that says, "Hey, I'm feeling good, and I'm sharing my joy with you!"

Then there are those moments when they puff up and sit quietly in a corner – this might look adorable, but it could mean they're feeling stressed or unwell. You know, kind of like when you're curled up on the couch, binge-watching your favorite series because you just need a break from the world. A budgie does the same thing, in their own way, when they're seeking solitude or comfort.

The key to understanding your budgie's behavior is to pay attention. I'm talking about noticing the little things: how they react when you approach their cage, whether they prefer to be handled or left to do their own thing, and what foods make them jump for joy. You'll start to notice patterns and quirks – a sort of *bird language* that's all your own. You'll learn to read them like an open book, and that connection? It's magic.

Chapter 1: Getting Started with Budgies

Before you go running off to your local pet store or adopting the cutest little budgie you can find online, let's hit pause for a second. You see, bringing a budgie into your life is not just about having a pretty little bird in a cage. It's about inviting a tiny, energetic ball of feathers into your home – and with that comes a bit of responsibility.

First things first: budgies are social creatures. They love company, attention, and interaction. So, if you're someone who's away from home a lot, or you can't spare a bit of time each day to give them some love, you might want to think twice. They're not like a goldfish that you can just feed and forget about (though, let's be real, even goldfish deserve better than that).

Budgies are also a bit like the class clowns of the bird world. They're playful, curious, and sometimes downright cheeky. They'll squawk for your attention, give you a side-eye when you don't pay them enough mind, and will probably end up flying around like they own the place. It's part of their charm, honestly. But if you're ready to embrace a bird that's got more personality than some people you know, then you're in for a treat.

Before you jump in, ask yourself: do you have the time, energy, and patience for a little feathery friend? If the answer is yes, then buckle up – you're about to experience the joys of budgie ownership.

Selecting the Right Budgie: Male or Female?

Now that you're on board, it's time to pick your budgie. This part can feel a little like matchmaking, honestly. You want to choose a bird that fits your vibe, right? The good news is, budgies – regardless of gender – are pretty similar when it comes to care. But there are a few little differences between males and females that might help you make your choice.

Males tend to be a bit more outgoing and vocal. They're the ones that will often whistle tunes, chatter away, and generally be the life of the party. If you're looking for a bird who's eager to chat (or sing), a male budgie might be the one to go for. Plus, they can be more affectionate, often bonding closely with their owners.

Females, on the other hand, can be a bit more independent and sometimes even a little more reserved. They're still social, don't get me wrong, but they might not be as vocal or as keen to interact all the time. In some cases, female budgies can also be a bit feistier, especially if they're feeling territorial. If you're into a more laid-back, "let me do my thing" kind of bird, a female might be your ideal match.

Of course, every budgie has its own personality, regardless of gender. But knowing these general traits can give you a little insight when making your decision. Either way, you're getting a bird with a ton of charm and character. Does that make sense?

Choosing the Best Cage for Your Budgie

Okay, you've picked your budgie – now it's time to think about where they're going to live. And let me tell you, budgies are like little gymnasts; they need space to spread their wings (literally). A cramped cage is no place for a creature that's designed to fly.

First rule of thumb: **bigger is always better.** I mean, you wouldn't want to live in a shoebox, right? Same goes for your budgie. A cage that's at least 18 inches wide and 18 inches deep is a good starting point, but the more room, the better. You want them to be able to stretch out, fly from one perch to another, and just feel comfortable in their home.

Next up: **bar spacing**. You don't want those bars too wide, or your budgie might escape or get stuck. Look for bars that are about ½ inch apart. This keeps them secure while still giving them enough room to climb and explore.

And don't forget about **accessories**. A few perches, some toys, and even a little mirror or bell can go a long way in making their cage feel like a cozy little retreat. Just make sure there's enough room for them to move around comfortably. The idea is to create a space where they can thrive – somewhere that feels like their little kingdom.

Essential Supplies for Your New Budgie

Okay, now that we've got the cage situation sorted, let's talk about the other things your budgie will need to be happy. There's no shortage of gadgets, gizmos, and doohickeys out there for budgie owners, but let's keep it simple with the essentials.

1. **Food and Water Dishes** – These are non-negotiable. You'll need sturdy dishes that won't tip over easily. Your budgie needs to stay hydrated, and a clean, fresh water supply is a must. As for food, you'll want to provide a balanced diet of seeds, pellets, and fresh veggies. More on that later, but it's important to make sure their food is nutritious.

2. **Perches** – Your budgie will need perches to rest on and stretch their little legs. Try to offer a variety of perches – some thicker for gripping, some thinner for their feet to flex. Natural wood perches are often the best choice since they mimic the branches of trees.

3. **Toys** – Yes, budgies love toys. Give them a few to keep them entertained – bells, swings, and

foraging toys are all good options. These help prevent boredom and keep their brains sharp.

4. **A Bird Bath** – Budgies love to splash around! You can get a small bird bath that attaches to the side of their cage, or you can even give them a gentle spritz with a spray bottle (just make sure it's lukewarm water).

5. **A Travel Cage** – If you plan on taking your budgie with you on trips, a small, portable cage is a must. It's also handy for trips to the vet.

Before you get all of this, though, take a step back and think about your budgie's personality. Will they be the type to love a swing or prefer a quiet corner with a simple perch? Are they into mirrors, or will they prefer a more natural, no-frills cage?

Chapter 2: Setting Up Your Budgie's Home

Okay, let's talk about where your budgie is going to call home. I'm not saying you need to roll out the red carpet or set up a penthouse suite, but a little thought goes a long way. The cage is where your budgie will spend a good portion of its time, so it's gotta be comfy, safe, and stimulating.

First off, size matters. You'll hear people say, "Bigger is better," and, honestly, when it comes to budgies, they're right. If you're aiming for a cage that gives your bird enough space to flap its wings, move around, and maybe even do a little spin when it's feeling particularly fabulous, you want to go bigger than the minimum. Look for something at least 18 inches wide, 18 inches deep, and 24 inches tall. It's not about luxury — it's about making sure your budgie has room to spread its wings without feeling cramped. You know, like a comfy couch versus a folding chair.

Where you put the cage is just as important. Budgies love a good view, so place the cage in a busy part of your home, but not in direct sunlight or drafty areas. Think of it like this: they want the front-row seat to the action, but they don't want to be blasted by a spotlight, either. Avoid putting the cage in the kitchen (hello, fumes!) or near a window where the temperature can fluctuate too much. And whatever you do, don't shove the cage in a corner like an afterthought. They're social creatures – your budgie wants to feel part of the family.

As for accessories, well, this is where things get fun. Perches, water bottles, food bowls, and toys – it's all part of the package. But, don't just grab any old thing. Think of it like designing a mini-playground for your bird. Variety is key: a few different perch types (wood, rope, etc.) and a couple of toys to keep things interesting. You can even throw in a mirror – because, yes, your budgie might just think it's got a second birdie friend hanging out with it.

Providing the Right Perches and Toys
You know how your budgie loves to flap around and stretch those little wings? Well, perches are the equivalent of a comfy armchair – they need to be supportive and varied to keep those tiny feet happy. A good rule of thumb is to have a mix of different-sized perches to mimic what they'd experience in the wild. You don't want your bird getting bored of sitting on the same plain wooden perch all day, right? Mix it up with natural branches (try to get ones that haven't been treated with pesticides), a rope perch for climbing, and maybe a swing for some added fun.

Toys are the secret sauce to keeping your budgie mentally stimulated and physically active. A bored budgie is a noisy budgie, and not in the "singing-you-a-song" way, but more in the "I'm-going-to-shout-until-you-notice-me" way. So, add a few toys that your bird can chew, climb, or ring (yes, those little bells are a huge hit). But, here's the kicker: make sure the toys are bird-safe. Avoid anything with small parts that could be chewed off or items with toxic materials. No one wants their budgie chewing on plastic that could harm it, right? If in doubt, go natural – wood, rope, and untreated materials are always a safe bet.

The Importance of Cage Cleanliness

Let's be real: no one likes living in a mess. Would you want to sleep in a room full of junk and old food wrappers? Neither would your budgie. Keeping the cage clean is one of those things that sounds like a chore, but once you get into a routine, it's honestly not too bad. Regular cleaning is essential for both your budgie's health and your sanity. A quick daily sweep to remove uneaten food, fresh water every day (trust me, your bird knows if it's stale), and a deeper clean once a week to wash down the bars, perches, and toys. It's a small investment in time that pays off in the form of a happier, healthier budgie.

And, let's not forget the cage tray – that little pull-out bottom where your budgie's…well, business, accumulates. You'll want to clean this regularly. A dirty cage is an unhappy cage, and a smelly one at that. Plus, budgies are pretty neat freaks by nature. If they see crumbs or droppings building up, it might stress them out. So, keep the place spick and span, and your budgie will thank you with sweet chirps and happy little hops.

Creating a Safe and Stimulating Environment

Okay, so you've got the basics down: cage, perches, toys, cleanliness. But what really ties everything together is creating an environment that's both safe *and* stimulating. We're talking about giving your budgie a space where it can truly thrive.

Start with safety first – check that the cage is sturdy and free from sharp edges that could hurt your bird. Avoid plastic or flimsy cages; budgies have strong beaks and sharp claws, and they'll use them to test just about everything. As for the rest of your home, keep it bird-proofed. Watch out for open windows, toxic plants, or things like non-stick cookware (that stuff is *deadly* for birds, seriously).

But, creating a stimulating environment isn't just about making sure your bird doesn't get into trouble. It's about encouraging natural behaviors, like foraging, climbing, and socializing. Try adding some branches to climb or hiding a treat in a toy to encourage your budgie to explore. Maybe even change things up occasionally – a new perch, a new toy, or a rearranged cage layout – just like you would redecorate a room to keep things fresh and interesting.

Remember: a happy budgie is one that has plenty of opportunities to engage with its world, not just sit in a cage waiting for you to notice. So, put a little thought into its environment – and before you know it, you'll have a happy, curious, and well-adjusted bird on your hands. Does that make sense? You want to create a space where your budgie can be its best self, just like you would for any other pet.

Chapter 3: Feeding Your Budgie

Let's get into the nitty-gritty of feeding your budgie. Picture this: you're at your favorite cafe, and the waiter brings you a plate of, well... everything. The works. You've got your proteins, carbs, veggies – the whole shebang. Now, would you just eat a pile of cookies and call it a day? I hope not. But when it comes to feeding our little feathered friends, a lot of us get caught up in just giving them seeds and thinking that's enough. Spoiler alert: it's not.

Budgies need a balanced diet just like we do. A good diet is key to keeping them healthy, happy, and full of energy. A mix of seeds, pellets, and fresh foods should be your go-to. Seeds are great as a base, but if that's all they're eating, it's kind of like feeding your child a steady diet of candy – fun, but not sustainable. You're going to want to make sure your budgie's plate is more like a rainbow than just one color.

A good rule of thumb is to offer about 60-70% of the diet as pellets (the good stuff that has all the vitamins and minerals they need) and the rest as seeds. A bit of fresh fruit, veggies, and the occasional treat, and you're golden. Does that make sense? Mix it up! Just like you wouldn't want to eat the same meal every day, your budgie doesn't either.

Recommended Seeds, Pellets, and Fresh Foods

Okay, so let's break down what actually goes into your budgie's food bowl. For seeds, you can't go wrong with a mix of high-quality millet, canary seed, and oats. They're a hit with budgies and pack some nutritional punch. But remember, variety is key! Try adding some spray millet or dandelion greens as a special treat – budgies go nuts for them.

Now, pellets are a bit of a must-have. Sure, your budgie might turn up its beak at first (because, let's be honest, they're picky little creatures), but trust me, they're worth it. Pellets are nutritionally balanced, so you can rest easy knowing your budgie is getting what it needs. Some brands even make them in different flavors, so you can cater to your budgie's "taste preferences." Yeah, it's like the bird version of a buffet.

And let's talk about the fresh stuff. Fresh fruits like apples, pears, and berries? Yes, please! Veggies like broccoli, carrots, and spinach? Even better. Your budgie will thank you for these little bursts of natural goodness, and you'll feel like a top-tier bird chef. Just make sure to avoid any citrus fruits or avocado – they're a no-go for budgies.

How to Set Up a Proper Feeding Schedule

Feeding a budgie is a bit like keeping a toddler on a routine. They like to know what's coming and when. So, let's get them on a schedule that works for both of you.

Start with two main feedings a day – one in the morning and one in the late afternoon. It's like the breakfast-and-dinner club, but for birds. Make sure they've got access to fresh water all day long, too. You can set out the food and let them nibble at their leisure, but don't leave it out for too long. Food that's left in the cage all day can get stale, and trust me, your budgie won't eat it – they're picky like that.

As for snacks? Sure, throw in a little treat now and then, but keep it in check. Treats are like the dessert of their diet – a fun extra, not the main course. So, no need to spoil them with too many sunflower seeds. I mean, they'll love you for it, but their waistline won't.

Treats and Supplements for Budgies

Speaking of treats... your budgie will definitely have its favorites, and that's where the fun begins. A bit of millet spray, a fresh sprig of parsley, or even a crunchy piece of carrot – they'll go wild for it. But, here's the thing: treats should always be a small percentage of their overall diet. A little goes a long way, and trust me, you don't want to end up with a bird who's spoiled and picky.

As for supplements? If you're feeding a balanced diet with pellets and fresh food, your budgie probably doesn't need much else. However, there are some good supplements out there, like cuttlebone (for calcium), or a mineral block. These helps keep their beaks and bones strong. It's like a little birdie multivitamin – you can't go wrong.

Keeping Your Budgie Hydrated

Last but certainly not least: water. I can't stress this enough – keep that water bowl fresh and clean. Budgies are like little water connoisseurs. If their water gets dirty or stale, they won't touch it. You can give them a water bottle, but I personally find that a bowl is better because it gives them more freedom to drink at will. Change the water every day, and maybe even give it a quick rinse to keep things squeaky clean.

It's easy to forget about hydration – we get so caught up in the feeding schedule, we might miss the fact that our feathered friend needs fresh water just as much as food. But trust me, a thirsty budgie is not a happy budgie.

Chapter 4: Grooming and Hygiene

Now, I know what you're thinking: "A bath for a bird? Seriously?" But bear with me — because just like us, budgies need a good rinse every now and then. And before you go grabbing the shampoo and a sponge, let me put your mind at ease: budgies don't need an elaborate spa treatment. In fact, it's all about simplicity.

Budgies love to bathe. In the wild, they'll splash around in puddles or take a dip in a fresh rain shower, so you want to give them the opportunity to do the same at home. All you really need is a shallow dish or a bird bath with just enough water to let them dip their little toes in and have a splash party. Place it in their cage or on a perch for easy access. Some budgies prefer a light misting of water from a spray bottle (nothing too heavy, though — we're not talking about a downpour here). Just make sure the water is lukewarm, not too cold or too hot. And honestly, some budgies are picky. They'll either dive in headfirst or look at the water like it's a puddle of doom. It's hit or miss — you'll figure out what your budgie likes with time.

You *don't* have to give them a bath every day. A few times a week is plenty, but if they start fluffing up their feathers and looking like they just rolled out of bed, it's a sign they're overdue for a rinse. Just make sure to let them dry off naturally afterward (no hairdryers, please). You want their feathers to stay healthy and fluffed up, not fried!

Nail Trimming: Step-by-Step Guide

Next up: nails. Now, if you've ever tried trimming a bird's nails, you know it's not exactly a walk in the park. It's more like trying to cut the nails of a tiny, squirmy acrobat who's determined to stay out of your reach. But don't worry, I've got your back.

Start by getting the right tools. You'll need a pair of bird-specific nail clippers or human nail clippers (the small ones, of course – no need to bring out the garden shears!). Make sure you're in a well-lit space, where you can see the nail clearly. Don't rush, take a deep breath. We're aiming for calm here – for both you and your budgie.

Now, here's the thing: budgies have a vein inside their nails called the "quick." If you cut into it, it can bleed – and that's a whole mess we want to avoid. So, only trim the sharp tips, avoiding the pink part of the nail. If you're unsure, start small and trim little by little. You can always take off a bit more later. And if you're feeling really nervous about it, you can always ask a vet to show you the ropes the first time.

And hey, if you mess up? Don't sweat it. You're learning, and your budgie will forgive you. Just keep a styptic powder or cornstarch on hand in case you nick the quick, and apply it to stop the bleeding. Pro tip: budgies often don't like their nails trimmed, so be prepared for some protest squawks. But it's for their own good, and once you're done, they'll thank you with a little more zooming around their cage.

Feather Care: Molting and Preening

Feathers — they're not just for show, you know. A budgie's feathers are like a built-in fashion statement, but more importantly, they're key to your bird's well-being. Keeping those feathers in tip-top shape is vital, so let's dive into how to care for them.

First, let's talk molting. If you've ever noticed your budgie shedding feathers like a mini snowstorm, don't panic. This is a normal process called molting, where your budgie sheds old feathers and grows in fresh, new ones. It's like a seasonal wardrobe change, except your bird doesn't get to pick out new outfits. Molting can happen a few times a year, and it usually lasts a couple of weeks. Your budgie might seem a little grouchier than usual, and you may find feathers all over your home (like confetti after a celebration). But hey, it's all part of the process.

Preening is another biggie. Budgies are the cleanest little creatures. They'll spend a good chunk of their day preening their feathers with their beaks, making sure every feather is in place and looking sharp. They'll even clean their beaks and feet while they're at it. If your budgie's preening too much, though — like, if you see bald spots or signs of over-grooming — it could be a sign of stress or health issues. So, keep an eye out.

But most of the time, preening is just a sign your budgie is taking pride in their plumage.

Keeping Your Budgie's Environment Clean

Now, onto the cage. Let's be real – nobody likes living in a mess, and that includes your budgie. Keeping their environment clean is just as important as feeding them the right food. No one wants to live in a dirty apartment, and your budgie's cage is their little slice of home, so it needs a little TLC.

Start by cleaning their food and water bowls daily. It's one of those things you'll just get used to, like brushing your teeth. Old food and dirty water are an invitation for bacteria, and we definitely don't want that. Wipe down the cage bars, too. Every week, empty the cage and give it a thorough scrub with warm water and a mild, bird-safe disinfectant. Pay attention to the corners where food crumbs and feathers collect. A clean cage makes for a happier, healthier budgie.

And don't forget about the floor of the cage – that's where the magic (or the mess) happens. It can get pretty gnarly with food bits, droppings, and the occasional feather explosion. Line the floor with safe, absorbent bedding (newspaper or paper towels work great). It'll help absorb moisture and make cleaning up a breeze.

In short: a clean cage means a happy budgie. And trust me, a happy budgie will repay you with chirps, songs, and maybe even a little dance.

Chapter 5: Understanding and Training Your Budgie

You've got your budgie settled in, the cage is perfect, and you've even got a nice little pile of seeds and fresh veggies ready for the feast. But here's the thing: it's not all about the snacks. Your budgie needs *you*. And no, I don't mean just throwing them some food every day and calling it a day. If you want your budgie to feel like part of the family, you've got to put in the time and effort to build a connection.

Imagine meeting a new person, and they're giving you the side-eye from across the room. How would you feel? Probably like they're not super interested in getting to know you. Well, that's kind of how your budgie feels when you don't engage. But don't worry — we can fix that! It's all about *patience* and *consistency*. Spend time near your budgie's cage talking to them in a calm, friendly voice. They might not respond at first, but with time, they'll start recognizing your voice and your presence. Trust me, they'll know when you're the one bringing the treats. Start slowly — don't rush things. Let them come to you when they're ready. Eventually, you'll see that cute little head tilt or that "what's up?" look they give you when you walk into the room. That's trust, baby.

Does that make sense? It's not about forcing the bond, it's about letting it grow naturally.

Basic Training Techniques: Step-by-Step

Now, onto the fun stuff: training! Budgies are smart little cookies, and they can learn all sorts of tricks. But here's the catch – they're not going to just do it because you ask. You've got to teach them, step by step, and the key is *positive reinforcement.* This means rewards, not punishment. Ever tried getting a dog to fetch a ball by yelling at it? Yeah, that doesn't work for birds either.

Start by teaching simple things. Like, getting your budgie to hop onto your finger. It sounds easy, but it might take a little patience. Start by holding your finger near their perch, and gently encourage them to step onto it. If they take the plunge, even for just a second, reward them with a treat. Remember, short training sessions are best – five minutes a day is plenty to keep things fun without overwhelming your feathered friend.

And don't forget, repetition is key. The more you practice, the more your budgie will pick up. Soon, you'll have a bird that's hopping on command, and maybe even doing a little dance for you (hey, it's possible).

Teaching Your Budgie to Talk

Okay, now for the showstopper: getting your budgie to talk. Yes, I said *talk.* I know it sounds like a long shot, but it's totally doable – with a little patience, of course. First thing's first: choose a word or phrase you want your budgie to learn. "Hello" is a great starter word, or you could go for something more fun like "Who's a pretty bird?" (They'll love the attention when they start saying it!)

Here's the trick: repetition, repetition, repetition. Say the word or phrase slowly and clearly whenever you interact with your budgie. Over time, they'll start associating the sound with the action. Don't expect them to start talking overnight – it can take weeks or even months depending on the bird, but once they get the hang of it, it's *so* worth it.

Side note: some budgies are natural chatterboxes, while others are more reserved. If your budgie isn't showing interest in mimicking, don't stress. Every bird's different. But, hey, if you can get them to whistle or chirp a few notes, consider that a win!

How to Handle Your Budgie Safely

Alright, we've bonded, we're training, and now it's time for handling your budgie. This is where things can get a little tricky. Budgies are small, delicate creatures, so you want to make sure you're handling them gently. Think of them like a tiny, feathery egg that can fly away at the drop of a hat.

To start, never grab your budgie by the wings or body – that's a no-go. Instead, let them climb onto your hand or finger on their own. If you're just starting out, let them perch on your finger while they get used to the feel of your hand. Gently guide them to your palm and give them a little scratch on the head – they love that. The more you handle them carefully, the more confident they'll feel. And if they fly away? Don't sweat it – just let them come back to you when they're ready. Like any relationship, you've got to give them the space to feel comfortable. You wouldn't rush into a hug with someone you just met, right?

Socializing Your Budgie with Other Pets

And now, the ultimate challenge: mixing your budgie into the pet family. If you have other pets – especially cats or dogs – you've got to take things slow. Budgies are small, and they're not always aware of the bigger creatures in the house, so the last thing you want is a tense standoff between your cat and your feathered friend.

Start by introducing your budgie to other pets at a safe distance. Keep the cage in a spot where your cat or dog can see them but not get too close. Over time, your pets will learn that the budgie is part of the family, too. Just make sure to always supervise any interactions. I mean, cats will be cats, and dogs will be dogs – they're naturally curious. But once your budgie starts to feel at ease around your other pets, they'll usually adapt. Just take it slow and never leave them unsupervised until you're 100% sure everyone can coexist peacefully.

Chapter 6: Health and Wellness

Let's get real for a moment – when you bring a little budgie into your life, you want them to be happy, healthy, and thriving. But how do you know if they're feeling *good*? After all, budgies can't exactly tell you in words, right? No "Hey, I'm feeling great today, thanks for asking!" So, you've got to become a bit of a bird whisperer. And don't worry – it's not as hard as it sounds.

A healthy budgie should be active, alert, and full of energy. They'll be flitting around their cage, chirping away, and generally looking like they're living their best life. You'll notice they're curious, pecking at toys, and showing interest in what's going on around them. Their feathers should be smooth, shiny, and not all ruffled up (unless they're just about to take a nap). Their eyes should be bright and clear, and you should see that little sparkle when they look at you. You know that feeling when you're with someone who's just *alive* and full of energy? That's what you're looking for in your budgie.

Also, pay attention to their droppings. Yeah, I know, not the most glamorous part of budgie care, but those little poops can tell you a lot about your bird's health. Healthy budgie droppings should be solid with a bit of white, urine-like substance. If you notice watery, overly dry, or discolored droppings, something's up.

Does that make sense? Healthy birds just give off this vibe – it's like when you walk into a room and instantly know someone's in a good mood. Trust your gut, you'll figure it out.

Common Budgie Health Issues and How to Spot Them

Okay, now that we know what healthy looks like, let's talk about the red flags – the things that might make you go, "Hmm, something's not right here."

One of the most common issues in budgies is *feather-plucking*. If your bird is suddenly nibbling at their own feathers or pulling them out, it could be a sign of stress, boredom, or even illness. Budgies are pretty clean little creatures, so if they're losing feathers, there's usually a reason behind it. You'll also want to keep an eye out for signs of *respiratory problems*, like wheezing or a discharge from the beak or nostrils. If you hear them making unusual sounds (almost like a whistle or a rattle when they breathe), that's a big red flag.

Another one to watch for is *diarrhea* or abnormal droppings. As I mentioned before, if their poop suddenly looks weird, it's a sign they might be unwell. Same goes for any changes in their eating or drinking habits – if your budgie starts eating or drinking a lot less than usual, don't ignore it.

Oh, and don't forget about *the beak*. If it looks uneven, cracked, or if your budgie is having trouble eating, something's not right. Keep a close eye on these little signs, and you'll be ahead of the game.

How to Prevent Illnesses in Budgies

Now that we know what to look out for, let's talk prevention. Because, honestly, the best medicine is keeping your budgie healthy in the first place, right?

Start with the basics: a clean environment. I know, I know, cleaning the cage is no one's favorite task, but trust me – it's worth it. A dirty cage can lead to bacteria and germs, which, surprise, isn't good for your budgie. Clean the cage, food bowls, and water containers regularly to avoid any potential problems.

Another key piece of the puzzle is a *balanced diet.* Just like us, budgies thrive when they're eating the right mix of nutrients. If you're feeding them a variety of seeds, pellets, and fresh fruits/veggies, you're already on the right track. Avoid overfeeding them too many seeds – it's like giving your kid a bowl of candy and expecting them to stay healthy. Mix it up! And don't forget about exercise – a budgie who's constantly flying around and hopping from perch to perch is going to stay healthier than one who spends all day just sitting there.

Finally, make sure your budgie gets plenty of mental stimulation. You wouldn't want to be stuck in a room all day with nothing to do, right? So, throw in some toys, new perches, or even a puzzle feeder. Give them something to think about. A bored budgie can easily turn into a stressed-out one, and that's not good for their health.

When to See a Veterinarian

Okay, so what happens when something *does* go wrong, and you're not sure what to do? Here's the deal: if you notice your budgie acting differently, don't wait around hoping it'll get better on its own. Birds, especially budgies, are masters at hiding their discomfort. They're little warriors, and they'll often act normal until things are really bad. So if your budgie is lethargic, not eating, having trouble breathing, or showing any other concerning signs, take them to the vet. *Don't* wait for it to get worse.

If you're not sure who to call, find a vet that specializes in avian care. Just like you wouldn't take your dog to a cat vet (doesn't make sense, right?), you want someone who knows birds inside and out. Budgies are delicate, and they need a vet who understands the ins and outs of bird care.

First Aid for Budgie Owners

Okay, here's where you need to be a bit of a first responder. I'm not saying you need to become a full-fledged avian paramedic, but it helps to know the basics.

First off, have some emergency supplies on hand — things like bandages, tweezers, and antiseptic. If your budgie gets a minor cut or injury, you'll want to clean the wound and stop any bleeding (but don't go full panic mode). If it's more serious, or if you're unsure, don't hesitate to call the vet immediately.

Another tip: if your budgie is choking or having trouble with food, *don't* try to do a Heimlich maneuver on them. Birds have delicate air sacs and can get hurt easily. Instead, contact a professional. Does that make sense? When it comes to first aid for birds, it's all about staying calm and knowing when to reach out for help.

Chapter 7: Breeding and Raising Budgies

Alright, so you're thinking about breeding your budgies. Before you dive in headfirst, let's just take a beat. Breeding budgies can be a magical experience – watching little chicks hatch and grow is like witnessing a mini miracle right before your eyes. But, and I say this with love, it's not for the faint of heart. It's a big commitment. Think of it like deciding whether or not you're ready to host Thanksgiving dinner for the whole family. Sure, it sounds fun and rewarding, but there's a *lot* of prep work involved.

You've got to be ready to provide proper care for both the parents and the babies. Breeding requires time, attention, and a solid understanding of your budgie's health and behavior. So, if you're not ready to juggle feeding, cleaning, and ensuring everyone's safe and healthy, it might be worth reconsidering. Does that make sense? Breeding is a huge responsibility, and you should only jump in if you're prepared for the work that comes with it.

Setting Up a Breeding Cage

If you've decided to go for it, then let's talk about the breeding setup. This is where things get serious, but don't worry — we'll keep it straightforward. The breeding cage needs to be a little different from the usual living arrangement your budgies have. You want to make sure it's spacious enough to give the pair room to move around but cozy enough that they feel comfortable nesting. Think of it like preparing the perfect "homey" environment for a couple who's getting ready to settle down.

Ideally, the cage should be about 24 inches wide, 18 inches deep, and 24 inches tall. You want to give the pair enough space, but also make sure it's not too big — you want them to feel safe and secure. Add a nesting box to one corner, and make sure it's positioned at a comfortable height. The box should be large enough for the hen to move around inside but not too big that she feels exposed.

Don't forget about the environment outside the cage, either. You'll want the breeding cage to be in a quiet area where the birds can feel undisturbed. No loud noises, no big parties. This is their time to focus on their new family, so give them some peace and quiet to do their thing.

How to Care for Budgie Eggs and Chicks

Once the eggs start showing up, things get real! Watching the hen lay her eggs is like watching a little piece of nature unfold right in front of your eyes. And let me tell you, that egg is fragile, like a little treasure. The first thing you'll need to do is make sure the eggs stay safe and warm. Most budgie parents will do a good job of incubating the eggs, but you'll still want to check in on them. Make sure the parents are both feeding and taking turns keeping the eggs warm. If the parents aren't doing their job, you might need to step in, but don't panic – there are ways to do this gently.

As for the chicks, once they start hatching (and you'll *know* when that happens, trust me), it's a whole new world. The chicks will be tiny little things at first, with eyes closed and feathers still forming. The parents will do most of the work, but you'll want to keep an eye on them to ensure they're all feeding and growing at a healthy rate. If you're feeling a bit anxious about their care, don't sweat it – just focus on keeping the environment calm, warm, and safe.

Raising Healthy and Happy Budgie Babies

Now, the real fun begins. Raising budgie babies is like being a proud parent – only with a lot more chirping and a lot less sleep. The chicks will need lots of food and attention from their parents at first, but after about 3 to 4 weeks, they'll start getting their feathers, hopping around, and making their way toward independence. And that's when the real joy happens: watching them take those first tentative steps toward the outside world.

As the babies start to grow, keep the environment clean and comfortable. Make sure they're getting enough fresh food and clean water, and keep an eye on them for any signs of distress. You'll want to be on the lookout for any health issues, as baby budgies are more sensitive than adults. But don't stress – if you've set up the right environment and are giving them plenty of care, the little ones should flourish.

You'll also need to start thinking about the socializing aspect of things. Budgies are social by nature, so once the babies are old enough, they'll be ready to start interacting with the world. This can include introducing them to other budgies, toys, and even your own family members. But be patient – socialization is a gradual process. You'll want to make sure they feel comfortable before throwing them into the social scene, sort of like introducing a new puppy to a bunch of people for the first time.

And there you have it. Raising budgie babies is a lot of work, but it's incredibly rewarding. Watching them grow, seeing them take their first steps, and eventually sending them off to their new homes (or keeping them in your flock) is a joy you won't soon forget.

Chapter 8: Troubleshooting Common Problems

Ow, the dreaded budgie scream! You know the one – it's that loud, shrill, "I'm-about-to-blow-your-eardrums-out" squawk that makes you wonder if the neighbors are starting to ask questions. We've all been there. But don't panic! There's usually a reason behind it. First things first, budgies are vocal creatures by nature. They *love* to make noise, and sometimes they just want to hear their own voices echoing back at them (sound familiar, right?).

But if the screaming is happening at all hours of the day or night, it might be a sign that something's off. Maybe they're bored and need more stimulation. Try adding a few new toys or changing up their environment a bit. Or maybe they're just trying to get your attention — because, let's face it, when you're sitting on the couch enjoying a Netflix binge, the last thing you want is to be interrupted by a shrieking bird. You know what I mean? So, make sure your budgie is getting enough interaction and playtime. It could also be a sign they're feeling lonely or stressed. Budgies are social animals, and if they're feeling isolated, they'll let you know loud and clear. A little attention and variety could be the perfect remedy for a screaming budgie.

Dealing with Feather Plucking

Okay, now onto something a bit more serious: feather plucking. If you've noticed your budgie yanking at their feathers or even leaving bald patches, don't brush it off as just a weird quirk. Feather plucking is a sign of distress — physical or emotional. It could be triggered by stress, boredom, or even medical issues. So, the first step is to rule out any health problems. If they're not sick, then it's time to look at their living conditions.

Is their cage too small? Are they lonely? Is there something in their environment that's making them anxious, like loud noises or too much commotion in the house? Sometimes, just making their home feel safer and more stimulating can stop the plucking. Think about it: how would you feel if you were stuck in a small room with nothing to do but stare at the same walls every day? Not great, right? Try giving them more space to fly, and add some perches and toys that can keep them occupied.

If feather plucking becomes a real problem, or it's affecting their health, it's time for a visit to the vet. Trust me, they're not going to judge you – they've seen it all. Better to get ahead of it than wait for it to get worse.

Aggressive or Shy Behavior: How to Manage It

Now, let's talk about behavior. If your budgie's been a little... well, *difficult,* you're not alone. Budgies, like people, have personalities. Some are bold and outgoing, while others are a little more reserved. But when that shyness turns into outright aggression, or the shyness becomes so extreme that they're not comfortable with anyone, it can become a problem.

If your budgie's showing aggression, it could be a sign of territorial behavior – they might feel like their cage is *their* space, and no one else is allowed in. If this is the case, back off a bit and let them come to you. Give them some space to relax. Aggression can also happen if your budgie feels threatened or scared. Try using a calm voice when approaching them, and make sure their environment is as stress-free as possible.

On the flip side, if you've got a super shy budgie who doesn't want to interact with you at all, the key is patience. Spend time sitting near them, talking to them in a soothing voice, and letting them get comfortable with your presence. Slowly build trust by offering treats, but don't rush it. Just like with people, trust takes time – you wouldn't ask a friend to spill their deepest secrets on the first meeting, right?

What to Do if Your Budgie Stops Eating

And then there's the worst-case scenario: your budgie stops eating. Suddenly, the little guy won't touch his food, and you're starting to panic, wondering if something's seriously wrong. First things first: check their health. A sudden loss of appetite can sometimes be a sign of illness, and it's one of those things you don't want to mess around with. Make sure to keep an eye on their behavior. Are they still drinking water? Are they lethargic or showing other signs of illness? If so, it's time to make a vet appointment. But if they're still active and alert, they may just be a bit finicky – budgies can get bored of their food, believe it or not!

Try offering a variety of different foods – fresh veggies, fruits, or even a new type of seed mix – just to see if something sparks their interest. Sometimes, a little variety is all it takes to get them back to their usual pecking and munching. Just don't try to force feed them. That'll only stress them out more. And if all else fails, trust your instincts – and remember, when in doubt, a visit to the vet never hurt anyone.

Chapter 9: Fun Activities for Budgies

Now dive into a fun part. Because, let's be honest, budgies are full of energy and curiosity, and they need more than just a perch and some food to stay happy. They're like little feathered toddlers – always exploring, always on the go. And the best part? You get to be their partner in crime!

So, how do you keep them entertained? Simple – *toys*. And I'm not talking about just any toys. Your budgie needs the good stuff – the kind that gets them thinking, playing, and flapping around like they've just discovered a treasure chest of fun. Think swings, ladders, and bells. Budgies love shiny things, so throw in a mirror or a toy with some colorful beads. And let's not forget about foraging toys – these are a game-changer. They love working for their food. A simple treat hidden in a puzzle toy will get your budgie so excited, you'll think they've won the birdie lottery.

The key here is variety. Switch things up every week to keep your budgie guessing. Imagine being stuck in a room with the same three toys forever – you'd probably get a little bored too, right? So, treat your budgie to something new every now and then. You'll see their excitement in full swing.

Does that make sense? The more you engage their minds and senses, the happier they'll be. They're not just little pets – they're companions with big personalities, and they deserve some fun!

How to Train Your Budgie to Do Tricks

Now that we've got them entertained, let's talk about *training*. Yep, you heard me – training your budgie can actually be fun (and you'll feel like a bird-whisperer in no time). Sure, they're not going to learn to juggle or do backflips (unless you're really lucky), but they can master some adorable tricks that will leave you both beaming with pride.

The trick to budgie training is patience, consistency, and, of course, treats. Start small – maybe with teaching your budgie to step up onto your finger. It's like training a dog, but cuter and less drooly. Hold out your finger, give them a gentle nudge (nothing too forceful), and when they step up, reward them with a treat or a bit of praise. Repeat, repeat, repeat. The more they realize they're getting a reward for certain behaviors, the quicker they'll catch on.

You can teach them to fly to your hand, wave a wing, or even "talk" (more on that later). The best part? Every time they learn something new, it feels like you've unlocked a new level in a video game. It's thrilling for both of you. So, don't be discouraged if it takes time. Remember, patience is key. Your budgie isn't going to perform tricks on demand overnight (unless you're some kind of magical bird trainer). But with some time and dedication, you'll be amazed at how much they can learn.

Letting Your Budgie Fly Freely (Safely!)

Now, onto something that will make both you and your budgie's hearts soar: *flying*. It's in their nature. Imagine being cooped up in a small room all day – wouldn't you want to spread your wings too? Budgies are born to fly, so giving them the chance to stretch those wings will make them feel like a million bucks.

But (you knew there was a "but" coming), flying freely indoors is a bit of an art form. You can't just open the cage door and hope for the best. No, no. You've got to be a bit more strategic about it. Start with small sessions in a room with few hazards – no ceiling fans, open windows, or other pets lurking around. Trust me, I've learned that lesson the hard way. They're fast little things, and before you know it, they're flying into every nook and cranny like they're auditioning for a role in "Mission Impossible."

To keep things safe, you can also get your budgie used to flying within a designated space by setting up a flight zone. Think of it like creating a safe playground for them. Open the door to their cage, let them perch on your hand, and then slowly encourage them to fly to a nearby perch or back to you. They'll get the hang of it in no time.

And hey, you'll probably find yourself running around the room, laughing as your budgie zips from perch to perch. It's one of those simple pleasures that never gets old.

Exploring Outdoor Cages and Aviaries

Okay, I know we've been talking a lot about indoor fun, but if you've got the space and the weather's right, it's time to talk about *outside* fun. Imagine your budgie basking in the sunshine, surrounded by fresh air and new sights. Sounds like paradise, right? Well, an outdoor cage or aviary can offer that.

But before you start setting up a five-star outdoor resort for your bird, keep in mind a few things. Safety is your number one priority. Make sure the aviary is escape-proof – budgies are escape artists, and if they see an opening, they'll take it. Also, keep an eye on the temperature and weather conditions. Too hot? Too cold? No good. You don't want your budgie to feel uncomfortable or exposed to the elements.

An outdoor aviary is a great way to let your budgie explore a bit more naturally while still keeping them safe. They'll get to feel the breeze in their feathers, hear the sounds of the outside world, and just generally enjoy life beyond the cage. Plus, it's a great way for you to sit back and watch your budgie channel their inner adventurer.

Chapter 10: The Lifespan of Your Budgie

Okay, let's have a heart-to-heart about your budgie's life expectancy. We all want our little feathered friends to live long, healthy lives, right? It's like having a small, precious spark of joy that you want to keep glowing for as long as possible. Well, the good news is that, with the right care, a budgie can live anywhere from 10 to 15 years (sometimes even longer if they're really spoiled – and let's be real, they probably will be).

How do you make sure your budgie gets the long and happy life they deserve? It's all about *balance.* You want to make sure they've got the essentials: a nutritious diet, daily mental and physical stimulation, and a clean, safe environment. You wouldn't leave a child in a room full of junk food, right? Same principle applies here – a balanced diet with a mix of seeds, pellets, and fresh veggies is crucial. It's the "food pyramid" of the bird world. And don't forget to give them plenty of time out of the cage to stretch those wings!

Here's the kicker: love and attention go a long way too. Budgies are social animals, and they thrive on companionship – whether it's with you, another budgie, or even a friendly cat (well, maybe not *too* friendly). Their mental well-being is just as important as their physical health. So, give them some quality one-on-one time, let them explore, and be sure to check in with their mental state as well. It's the little things that add up, and before you know it, you'll be looking at your budgie and thinking, "Wow, we've made it through so many great years together."

Does that make sense? The key is consistency – a little love, a little care, and a lot of patience. Simple stuff, but it works wonders.

The Aging Budgie: Signs to Watch For

Okay, now, as much as we'd love to freeze time and keep our budgies young forever (wouldn't that be great?), the reality is, just like us, they get older. And as they do, their needs change. So, how do you know when your budgie is entering their golden years? It's like when you notice the first gray hairs creeping in – it's not always easy to spot, but when you do, you have to start paying a little extra attention.

First off, older budgies tend to slow down a bit. They might not be as chirpy or zippy around the cage, and they might prefer relaxing on a perch rather than darting around. Their feathers could also become a bit duller or more ragged. You know how you can sometimes feel the difference between your twenties and your thirties (or forties… or fifties, depending on how much sleep you've been getting)? Budgies go through a similar shift. Their bodies start to wear down just a little, and it's important to keep an eye on that.

Other signs of aging include changes in their eating habits, more sleep, and maybe even a bit of grumpiness. Not all budgies will show it, but some might start to get a little more territorial or picky about who's allowed to interact with them. It's kind of like when your grandma starts hiding her chocolate stash – they just want things on their terms!

Does that make sense? Aging is natural, but it can be hard to spot the first signs. Keep your eyes peeled, and make sure your budgie's needs are still being met, even as they start to mellow out.

How to Help Your Budgie Through Its Senior Years

Alright, so your budgie is getting older – now what? First things first, don't panic. With a little TLC, they can live out their golden years comfortably and happily. As they age, they may need a little extra help, and you'll want to adjust their environment to make things easier on them.

For one, you might want to add some more comfy perches. Those old perches you've had for years? They might not be as cushy as they used to be. Try adding some soft, easy-to-grip perches made from materials like rope or cotton – something that's a little gentler on their feet as they get older.

Also, consider their diet. Older budgies can sometimes have a harder time chewing harder seeds or pellets. Try offering them softer foods, like mashed veggies or fruit – things they can easily nibble on without straining their beaks. And make sure they're drinking plenty of water too. You'd be surprised how easy it is for birds to get dehydrated, especially as they age.

In terms of socializing, let them take the lead. Some older budgies prefer a quieter environment, so respect their space if they seem a little less social. On the flip side, others might get cuddlier in their senior years. Go with the flow and let them guide you.

And don't forget regular vet checkups. Just like we go for those yearly physicals, your aging budgie should have regular visits to the vet to keep an eye on any potential health problems. They might need a little extra care, but trust me, it's worth it when you see them hopping around happily, living their best retired life.

You know what I mean? Aging doesn't have to mean slowing down. With some thoughtful adjustments and a lot of love, your budgie can live out their senior years with just as much joy as they had when they were younger.

Enjoying Life with Your Budgie

We've come to the end of this little budgie journey. But don't worry, it's just the beginning of your *real* adventure with your feathered friend. If you've followed all the tips and tricks (and let's be honest, probably spoiled your budgie a little along the way), you're now ready to enjoy a long, happy life together. And trust me, you're in for a treat. Budgies are charming, quirky, and full of surprises – they'll make you laugh, smile, and occasionally scratch your head in wonder at their antics. You know those days when you come home from work, feeling exhausted, and then your budgie hops onto your shoulder like, "Hey, I missed you"? That moment, right there, is everything.

But it's not just about the laughs and the cute moments. It's about the bond you build. Living with a budgie means living with a little personality that will *grow* on you – and you on them. It's that subtle shift from "just a pet" to "a little companion" who shares your space and your heart. They'll start to recognize your voice, anticipate your routine, and maybe even get a little cranky when you're late feeding them (not that I would know from personal experience). That's the magic of having a budgie – they're not just birds; they're little souls with big hearts.

Building a Long-Term Bond with Your Parakeet

But here's the thing about long-term relationships – they take time, effort, and a whole lot of trust. The bond you share with your budgie will grow deeper the more you invest in it. Spend time talking to them, even when you think they're not paying attention. Budgies are more observant than we give them credit for. And, of course, *patience* is key. If they're not taking to their training right away, don't throw in the towel. Like any good friendship, it takes time to figure out the rhythms of each other's needs and quirks.

Your budgie will look to you for everything – safety, food, fun, and affection. And in return, they'll offer you their *true* selves: that unique chirp, the bright flash of color, and, eventually, the joy of hearing them mimic your voice or whistle your favorite song. It's these moments, small but significant, that turn a pet into a part of the family. You're not just taking care of a bird; you're growing a relationship that, over time, will feel as effortless and comfortable as breathing.

Does that sound like a dream? It's not – it's just the reality of living with a budgie.

Final Tips and Resources for Budgie Owners

Before I let you go, let me leave you with a few parting words of wisdom.

First, remember that every budgie is different. Sure, they're all adorable, social creatures, but just like people, they each have their own personalities, likes, and dislikes. Don't expect them to all behave the same way – if yours prefers to watch you from a distance for a while before becoming a lap bird, that's totally okay. Give them space and time, and you'll see their true colors shine through.

Second, never underestimate the power of *routine*. Budgies are creatures of habit. They feel safer when they know what to expect, so try to keep feeding times and playtime predictable. You'll notice how much more relaxed and comfortable they are when they know what's coming next.

Lastly, always be on the lookout for new ways to enrich their lives. Whether it's a new toy, a new perch, or simply a change of scenery, budgies thrive when their environment is dynamic. After all, variety is the spice of life, right? It's true for us, and it's definitely true for your budgie. So, get creative and have fun with it!

And finally, don't forget – if you ever need a little extra help or advice, there are tons of resources out there. Bird forums, YouTube videos, and even vet consultations can offer valuable insights and guidance as you navigate life with your feathery friend.

There you have it. Your journey as a budgie owner is just beginning, and I promise, it's going to be a wild, wonderful ride. Here's to many years of chirps, cuddles, and endless joy with your budgie. Enjoy every moment – they're worth it.

Now go on, give your budgie a little head scratch from me!

Appendix

So you've got your budgie – now what? Well, there's no shortage of resources to help you become the best budgie parent you can be. Whether you're looking for expert advice, online communities, or just want to dive deeper into the fascinating world of budgies, here are some goldmine resources to keep you in the know.

Recommended Budgie Resources: Websites, Books, and Forums

1. **Websites**
   - **The Budgie Information Center** – A treasure trove of knowledge, this site covers everything from basic care to breeding. Bookmark it now. Seriously.
   - **BirdChannel** – This one's a great go-to for both general bird care and budgie-specific tips. It's like having a virtual bird care expert at your fingertips.
   - **Avian Web** – You can't go wrong here. Whether you're looking to understand your budgie's behavior or want tips on training, this site has you covered.
2. **Books**
   - *The Budgie Handbook* by Jenny R. Rains – A fantastic guide for beginner to advanced

budgie owners. It's clear, concise, and easy to follow. Perfect for when you want a little extra reading material while sipping coffee.

- *Budgies For Dummies* by Nikki Moustaki – Don't be fooled by the title – this book is packed with solid advice for budgie care. Plus, it's written by a seasoned bird expert, so you know it's legit.
- *The Parakeet Handbook* by Robyn J. Eversole – If you're a fan of practical, hands-on tips, this one's for you. It covers everything from diet to training, with a special emphasis on keeping your budgie entertained.

3. **Forums**
   - **Budgie Board** – A dedicated online community where fellow budgie owners chat, share tips, and swap stories. It's like the virtual version of sitting in a café, talking birds.
   - **BirdForum** – A broader site for all bird lovers, but the budgie section is packed with useful advice. Great for when you're trying to troubleshoot or get some quick feedback on a question.
   - **Reddit's r/budgies** – If you're a Reddit fan, this subreddit is a wonderful place to find tips, funny videos, and general budgie love.

Whether you're a newbie or an experienced budgie owner, these resources are your new best friends. The more you learn, the more you'll appreciate the little quirks and joys that come with sharing your life with a budgie.

Emergency Budgie Care Kit Checklist

We all hope it never happens, but it's always a good idea to be prepared for an emergency. Here's a quick checklist for an emergency care kit, just in case the unexpected pops up. It's like having a first-aid kit for your feathered friend.

- **Emergency bird carrier** – A small, well-ventilated cage that can fit your budgie comfortably.
- **Towel or cloth** – For gently restraining your budgie if needed (they'll appreciate the soft touch).
- **First aid supplies** – Tweezers, bandages, and sterile gauze.
- **Buddy for consultation** – Keep the phone number of an avian vet on hand. Trust me, it's a lifesaver.
- **Pedialyte** – In case your budgie gets dehydrated, this electrolyte solution can make all the difference.
- **Basic medications** – You won't need a full pharmacy, but having a couple of general bird-safe meds is a smart move (ask your vet for recommendations).

Keep your emergency kit somewhere easy to access but out of sight. It's one of those "better safe than sorry" deals. And remember, knowing what to do in an emergency is just as important as having the right supplies. Be sure to educate yourself on the basics of budgie first aid too – it's something no owner should overlook.

Budgie Health Record Template

Keeping track of your budgie's health is like keeping a diary for them. It's not just about remembering when they had their last check-up – it's about creating a roadmap of their wellness, so you can spot any changes or issues early on. Here's a simple health record template to help you stay organized:

Budgie Health Record

Name: _____
Age/Date of Birth: _____
Species: _____

Veterinary Check-ups:
Date of Visit: _____
Reason for Visit: _____
Vet's Notes: _____
Diet Changes:
Date: _____
Change in Diet (e.g., new food, added supplements):
_____

Behavioral Changes:
Date: _____
Observed Changes (e.g., excessive preening, lethargy, loss of appetite): _____

Molting and Feather Health:
`tart Date of Molt: _____
 ⅃ Date of Molt: _____
    `er Issues (if any): _____

Medications/Treatments:
Date Given: _____
Medication/Treatment: _____
Dosage: _____

Having this record on hand makes it easier for you to notice when something's off. And if you ever need to talk to a vet, you can just whip out the info like a pro. It's all about being proactive and making sure your budgie gets the care they need.

Printed in Dunstable, United Kingdom